A Guide For Godparents

By Peter C. Garrison

C.S.S. Publishing Company, Inc.
Lima, Ohio

A GUIDE FOR GODPARENTS

Copyright © 1991 by
The C.S.S. Publishing Company, Inc.
Lima, Ohio
Second Printing 1992

9127 / ISBN 1-55673-294-5   PRINTED IN U.S.A.

To Joanne.
To Jack and Aaron, our Godsons.

ACKNOWLEDGEMENTS

Thank you to Mr. Bill Marshall for his thoughtful help through "slash and burn" editorial suggestions. Thank you to The Rev. Kemp Segerhammer for his theological insights to God's fullness. Thank you to a university roommate of long ago, Mr. Gregory Villard, for making me feel like a writer. Thank you to the maternal insights of Ms. Jan Brewster and Ms. Karen Noble. To Joanne, my heart, all my thankful love.

TABLE OF CONTENTS

THE PURPOSE OF THIS BOOK

Dear Godparent:

The purpose of this book is to introduce the godparent to the joys and duties of the spiritual care of his or her godchild.

Godparents or prospective godparents will find this book helpful because it outlines specific Christian teachings on the meaning of baptism. The duties of the godparent are also explained. And the commitment of the church to the care and strengthening of godparents and their godchildren is also discussed.

This book will be especially helpful to the godparent who lives some distance from his/her godchild.

HOW TO USE THIS BOOK

Dear Godparent:

This book is addressed to you and your loving concern for your godchild, whether your godchild is indeed a child or an adult.

This book will involve you in the joy of your godchild's spiritual journey as well as lead you to examine your own life as a baptized child of God.

The basic baptismal truths of the Christian church will be addressed in this book. Ideas and prayers will be shared with you so that you may be faithful and effective in your duties as a godparent.

Although many of your questions as a godparent will be answered in this *Guide For Godparents*, the mysteries of God will remain mysteries. Therefore, as you live your life of faith, you will want to avail yourself of the community of saints; your local Christian church. This community of fellow believers will help you remain steadfast in your spiritual life with your living God. Also, you will want to visit with your pastor or priest or learn the fine points of your tradition's understanding of God's love shown to you and your godchild through baptism.

Here is how you can use this *Guide For Godparents:*

1. Read a part of this book.

2. Look up the Bible references in parentheses.

3. Read the quote in its Bible setting.

4. Then, quietly think over what you have read.

5. Picture yourself responding to what you have read as you live in your relationship with God and in your relationship with your godchild.

6. Next, ask God to help you as you minister to your godchild.

7. Finally, do something for your godchild that very moment based on your reading and prayers, scripture and reflection. For example: Pray for your godchild, write your godchild a letter, send her or him a Christian gift, telephone your godchild.

8. Discuss with your pastor any questions you may have.

God bless you and keep you and your godchild in his grace, through Christ Jesus.

Peter Garrison
Burlingame, California 1990

INTRODUCTION

Hooray, you are a new godparent! Or maybe you are about to become a godparent. Congratulations! But what does it mean to be a godparent? This book will help you see God's view of the situation. And, for you to see things from God's point of view is what baptism and being a godparent is all about.

Like all godparents, you are committed to being a faithful godmother or godfather to your godchild. You know that baptism is not simply a "naming ceremony," or merely a reason to get dressed up and have a pretty party at the neighborhood church. You know that something important is happening. You are reminded that you, too, are baptized.

But maybe you are a little hazy on just what the holy sacrament of baptism does for you and your godchild. Maybe you haven't been to church for awhile and were surprised when you were asked to be a godparent. Probably the parents or the pastor gave you this little book to help you understand the wonderful relationship you will have with your godchild in the eyes of God.

This book will cover the basics of what God does in baptism. This book will show you what you can do with your godchild as you both live in the joy of God's love. His love is given for you through Christ in the holy sacrament of baptism.

Nervous? Don't worry. Remember that God is love, that He loves you, and that we know this truth through Christ Jesus. "Do not be afraid," he says, ". . . for your Father has been pleased to give you the kingdom (Luke 12:32)."

We are given assurance of this kingdom through our baptism. Through God's love in baptism, we may live with our loving God forever in his kingdom. Let's find out more about this greatest of gifts: the love of God given to us through baptism.

13

Part One
WHO GOD IS
WHO YOU ARE

In Part One, we will review who God is, and who you are. This basic knowledge will be your foundation of loving godparenting.

Who God Is

The word "who," is important in understanding God. "Who" is a clue that God is known as a person. God is not a thing (a statue, a tree, or piece of crystal) or a place (a mountain or hidden wood). "I am who I am," declares God to Moses (Exodus 3:14).

God is pure "personhood," pure being and cannot be manipulated as if he were a magic formula or good luck charm. God is a "who." God seeks a living relationship with us and shows us who he is and what God wants through his Son Jesus.

Jesus himself was baptized. At Jesus' baptism the Holy Spirit descended upon him in the form of a dove. God the Father's voice was heard declaring, "This is my beloved Son, with whom I am well pleased (Matthew 3:16-17)."

Just a note at this point: God the Father, Jesus his Son, and the Holy Spirit are all one and the same God. A lot has been written about this mystery, and it remains a mysterious truth that we worship one true God who reveals himself in three persons. The main connection is that he is always revealed as love.

God the Father creates us in love. God the Son, who becomes truly human in Jesus, lovingly shows us God's will

15

in ways that we humans can readily understand. God the Holy
Spirit guides our hearts to trust Jesus and to believe in the God
he is: the God who rescues us from sin and death and gives
us eternal life because he loves us (John 3:16).

Now, to continue with who God is: We know who God
is through his Son, Jesus. Jesus shows us God's will by loving
us so much that he takes on our sin and dies the death our
sins demands. (We don't have to die forever, now that Jesus
has died for us.) Jesus shows us God's will by being raised
from the dead and ascending to God in heaven. God's will,
which is shown to us in Jesus' life, death and resurrection,
is to love God with all our "self" and to love our neighbor
as our "self."

Self-giving is the message of Christianity. God gives himself to us in baptism. We give ourselves to God and to our
neighbor when our lives are filled with the baptismal love of
God. "We love because he first loved us (1 John 4:19)."

In summary: When we ask, "Who is God?", we find the
answer in Jesus. ". . . God is love," writes John. "And in
this the love of God was made manifest among us, that God
sent his only Son into the world, so that we might live through
him (1 John 4:8b-9)."

Who Are You?

*God became like us when he became human in Jesus, so
that we might become like Jesus and live with God's love
forever.*

This paraphrase is from an early Christian writer who shows
us who we are, (or rather who we become) through our faith.
In baptism, we are shown to be sons and daughters of God,
"and if sons, then heirs," writes Paul (Romans 8:15b-17).

What we inherit as heirs is God's promise to be our God
and we to be his people. We are empowered by God to devote
ourselves to God as his obedient children. God gives us his

Holy Spirit to keep us selfless rather than selfish in our concerns.

Paul writes about daily turning from our self-centeredness and our rising to selfless concern for others when he notes: "We were buried therefore with him by baptism into death, so that as Christ was raised from the dead by the glory of the Father, we too might walk in newness of life. So you also must consider yourself dead to sin and alive to God in Christ Jesus (Romans 6:4, 10)."

Who you are is a child of God who has the hope of living forever. This is possible only because of who God is and what he has done for you through Jesus. Each of us may live lives of loving obedience to God, free from fear and death.

We never have to be afraid of death. We never have to run in fear from God. Our obedience to God comes from a loving thanksgiving to God who has given us so much — even eternal life! We can read Paul again: "For you did not receive the spirit of slavery to fall back into fear, but you have received the spirit of sonship (and daughterhood). When we cry, 'Abba! Father!' it is the Spirit himself bearing witness with our Spirit that we are children of God . . . (Romans 8:15-16)."

A question now: Where and when are we assured that we have this Spirit bestowed upon us so that we know we are children of God? You guessed it! In the holy sacrament of baptism.

In summary: God is love. You are beloved of God. The holy sacrament of baptism is a sign of this love of God for you. Through your own baptism you start a life long, indeed eternal loving relationship of serving God and loving others for his sake. You won't magically live a "better" life. But you will have the promise of God to be with you no matter what. You will be empowered to live in this loving relationship and to cooperate with the Holy Spirit in good works pleasing to God.

Part Two
THE HOLY SACRAMENT OF BAPTISM

In Part Two, we examine the holy sacrament of baptism and what it means in God's loving purpose for our lives; lives we can live with him, now and forever.

The three words: holy — sacrament — and baptism, will instruct us in discovering the goodness brought to us in this gift from our Heavenly Father.

Holy

The word holy means "separated to." "Separated to" sounds odd to us because we are familiar with the phrase "separated from." But in the ancient Greek word, *hagios,* we hear the ancient Greek custom of people dedicating themselves to their gods by separating themselves from concerns of worldly matter. In their separation "from" the world they were, in effect, separating themselves "to" their pagan gods.

The holy, in holy sacrament of baptism, means that what occurs in the sacrament is dedicated to God. The one who is baptized is called to be holy; that is, dedicated and set apart in order to serve God.

Holiness is not something we do. Holiness is a fact of being called into relationship with our Creator who is holy, set-apart, other-than the creation and yet in it.

Peter reminds us in his first letter, that, ". . . as (God) who called you is holy, be holy yourselves in all your conduct; since it is written, "You shall be holy, for I am holy (1 Peter 1:14)."

Holiness then, is not going around town acting like some saint in a Hollywood film. It is an awareness, "in all our conduct" that we are to be "obedient children" of God as we live a real relationship with a real God in the real world. We are to obey Christ's great commandment, "You shall love the Lord your God with all your heart and with all your soul, and with all your mind . . . You shall love your neighbor as yourself (Matthew 22:37-39)." We are in the world, but not of it. We are sojourners, caretakers of God's good creation.

We are to love because our God is love. God gives us this love through the sacraments.

Sacrament

A famous Christian, in the 300s, named Augustine, called a sacrament, "A visible sign of an invisible gift from God." A sacrament is like an object lesson from God for his children. Being mortal with our five senses of touch, smell, hearing, tasting and seeing, we learn more readily when these senses support our ability to reason. God sent his Son Jesus as a sign of his love; a real human sign who is also God himself. Because God becomes human in Jesus, we know better the wonder of God's love for us. We know also that he understands our temptations and sorrows.

God continues to send us his gifts of love and forgiveness in ways we can readily understand. Our senses are awakened and stimulated through the written word of the Bible that we hear and read, in the bread and wine we feel, taste, and smell during the sacrament of holy communion, and in the sound of God's forgiveness declared by a pastor or other Christian. God thus shows us his love in tangible ways.

The splashing water and the promise of God's Word in the sacrament of baptism shows our senses the cleansing, forgiving and refreshing aspects of God's presence in our new lives as children of God. We are "born from above," or "born again (John 3:5)."

In the 1500s, the theologian, Martin Luther, knew that we could find God wherever we are. But he reminds us that we don't have to buzz around looking for God everywhere like a bumblebee looking for honey. Rather, God comes to meet us in his Son, and he continues to meet us in his sacraments wherever they are celebrated in God's love.

We celebrate God's sacraments with his people gathered in his presence in church. This is the main reason why you, as a godparent, will help see to it that your godchild attends church: so that he or she will be in God's presence with God's people.

It is in the community of saints that your godchild will learn how to, "love the Lord your God with all your heart and with all your soul and with all your mind . . . (and) love your neighbor as yourself (Matthew 22:37-39)." This is a summary of God's will for us shown throughout the entire Bible.

Your godchild will receive great strength for his or her faith through the sacraments and through the people celebrating the sacraments in Jesus' name. Eternal life is offered to your godchild through the sacraments and can be called, as Ignatius called them long ago, "Medicine for the resurrection." Continued study of the Bible in Sunday school and church will keep your godchild aware of God's love and part of the community that celebrates and shares this love.

A sacrament then is a gift of God, made present to us in a way we can understand and celebrate. A gift of God is always a gift of love for the sake of loving God and neighbor.

We've looked at holy and sacrament to better understand God's blessings through baptism. Now we look at the word, baptism.

Baptism

Baptism is another ancient Greek word used in the New Testament. It means, "to dip" or "submerge" and comes from the idea of dipping clothes into dye again and again.

Some churches baptize people by gently laying them down in water and then lifting them up again. The mind's-eye picture of being laid down in water is like that of being laid down in a grave. Being raised again from the water is like being raised again from the dead. Other churches do not submerge the godchild fully in water. Some sprinkle water on the godchild or pour the water over the child or adult.

Regardless of the method used, the baptism is celebrated with water and Jesus' words. Baptism remains an action that shows us the truth of God's promise to love us now and forever by joining us to Jesus' baptism, Jesus' death and Jesus' resurrection. Baptism is also more than a demonstrative action — it is an act of God's love which really does join us to Jesus' death and thus into freedom from death through his resurrection.

When the waters of baptism splash on the godchild, the idea of being splashed clean is an important picture to keep in our mind's-eye. In baptism our sins are washed away. Now we can live forever with him as we live believing in Jesus' life, death and resurrection and following his ways of self-giving love.

You might ask, "How can water do such great things?" Martin Luther asked the same question in the 1500s. His reply is that, "It is not water that does these things, but God's Word with the water and our trust in the Word. Water by itself is only water, but with the Word of God it is life-giving water which by grace gives the new birth through the Holy Spirit."[1]

Paul writes in Titus 3: "He saved us . . . in virtue of His own mercy, by the washing of regeneration and renewal in the Holy Spirit, which He poured out upon us richly through Jesus Christ our Savior, so that we might be justified by His grace and become heirs in hope of eternal life."

It is helpful to keep in mind that ancient Greek picture of dipping garments into the dye again and again. The picture of dipping the godchild into the water and Word again and

---

[1] *The Small Catechism in Contemporary English* by Martin Luther. Copyright 1960 by Augsburg Publishing House, page 15

22

again is important for our understanding of what baptism means for our everyday lives.

It doesn't mean that we are to keep dunking the child each Sunday into the baptismal font. But all of us, as children of God, are to daily remember our baptism and live lives worthy of being called God's children. The Holy Spirit, our divine counselor and friend-in-the-faith, will give us the power to daily continue as children of God. "By this we know that we live in him and he lives in us, because he has given us of his own Spirit (1 John 4:13)."

Day by day, we recall our baptism and live loving lives. Luther defines our "daily" baptism this way: "It means that our sinful self, with all its evil deeds and desires, should be drowned through daily repentance; and that day after day a new self should arise to live with God in righteousness and purity forever."[2]

And how can we possibly live this life with God? Where will we find the strength and hope and courage for this challenge? Look closely at the way Luther describes our relationship begun with God through baptism. He writes that it is made so through, "God's Word with the water and our trust in the Word." It is through God speaking to us individually and enabling our response to his call that we are made children of God.

God promises in our baptism to be responsible for us. And in our baptism we are given the response-ability of thanking him with praise and adoration while we love our neighbor as ourself.

We will be exploring this idea of God acting and our reacting to him in the following chapters.

In summary: Part Two has introduced you into the "big picture" of baptism. The following parts of the book will give you the basic "How To's" of being a faithful godparent through your own baptism and your relationship with God.

---

[2](ibid).

23

Part Three

I'VE BEEN ASKED TO BE A GODPARENT!
WHAT'S GOING TO HAPPEN WHEN I SAY, "YES"?
WHAT HAPPENS AT THE BAPTISM?

I've Been Asked To Be A Godparent!

It may be a bit of a surprise to see yourself in the really quite exalted position of godparent. You may have already celebrated the happy event, or it may be coming up in the near future. You might be asking yourself, "How did I get into this anyway?" That's an important question to ask, because the answer is more wonderful than you might at first realize.

The basic answer to your question, "How did I get into this anyway?" is: "You were asked." But by whom were you asked?

In any relationship, human or divine, at least two persons are involved. In a sacramental relationship, Jesus is involved, too. You might say that the godchild's natural mom and dad asked you. Or you might see the greater reality that God is hearing the promises you make in his name during the sacrament of holy baptism. God, as well as the child's earthly parents, and the church, are asking you for your "pledge of good faith."

What you are doing is done in God's name. You are to be holy as your Lord God is holy. As you gather in his name and call on his name, he hears you and knows your heart.

You as a godparent are a witness to God's promise to your godchild. You are a helper in guiding your godchild's life in trusting God's promises until Jesus returns to bring his kingdom to perfect loving completion.

What you promise to do as a godparent may or may not be written down for you to say during the actual celebration

25

of the sacrament. But whether or not you read these or similar words, they outline the responsibility you have to your godchild:

"You should therefore faithfully bring them to the services of God's house, and teach them the Lord's Prayer, the Creed and the Ten Commandments. As they grow in years, you should place in their hands the Holy Scriptures and provide for their instruction in the Christian faith, that, living in the covenant of their Baptism and in communion with the Church, they may lead godly lives until the day of Jesus Christ."[1]

Any relationship, human or divine, is based on trust; a faith upon which you live your life. What is important in the sacrament of baptism is God's promise to your godchild, because God's promise is always true. You may succeed or fail as a godparent, but God always is true in his promise to be your godchild's heavenly father.

If you are worried about "failure" as a godparent, remember that your "responsibility" is a "response-ability" given to you through the strength and love of God. Your "ability" as a godparent depends upon a "response" worked in you through the Holy Spirit. You need not worry about failure as a godparent. Keep asking for strength and love in Jesus' strong name. God will keep his promise to be your God for both you and your godchild.

Remember to teach your godchild this fact: God always keeps his promise to be your godchild's personal God. That may be the most important thing your godchild will learn from you.

What's Going To Happen When I Say "Yes"?

"Yes!" is a reply that we cannot, on our own, say to God. As a matter of fact, we can only say, "No" to God when

---

[1] *Lutheran Book of Worship*, Augsburg Publishing House, Minneapolis. Holy Baptism, p. 121

we rely on ourselves alone to make a decision concerning our spiritual lives. This is because of our sinful natures. By nature, we do not want to listen to God or trust his promises.

For example, we hear the truth, "God is love (1 John 4:8)." Our typical human reaction is to say, "No, I don't think so. Look at how I am not as rich as I would like to be. Look at the suffering I go through. Look at how hard my boss is to get along with. Life could be better for me if God let me run the world my way. No, God is not love because I do not have everything I want."

As is obvious from above, we doubt God because we want to be number one in creation. We want to be God and not his image, or number two. We fail to see that God's love is a love we have to share and not hoard to our own benefit. This failure to see the fullness of God's love is a result of our sinful nature. And that is why we cannot, on our own, say, "Yes" to God's love without his loving help through the Holy Spirit.

How then can we say "Yes"? How can we be saved by believing in Christ, who, after all, is God's Word of promise in the flesh?

What a loving God requires, he supplies. He gives us the faith we need to trust Jesus as our Lord. He gives us our faith freely.

What God requires of us is to trust Jesus. How does God supply this faith? Through the "comforter," the Holy Spirit which proceeds from the Father and the Son: "I (Jesus) will pray the Father, and he will give you another Counselor, to be with you forever, even the Spirit of truth, whom the world cannot receive, because it neither sees him nor knows him; you know him, for he dwells with you, and will be in you . . . But the Counselor, the Holy Spirit, whom the Father will send in my name, he will teach you all things, and bring to your remembrance all that I have said to you (John 14:16, 26)."

You then, dear godparent, have said, "Yes" to God who is acting in your life. Is the Holy Spirit guiding you now? I hope so. May you recognize, too, the Comforter at work in your heart as you say a personal "Yes" to God's loving you in Jesus.

Soon you will join in the celebration of the sacrament of holy baptism. A sacrament is always a celebration because God in his love is truly present. You may be nervous or you may feel unworthy. But remember, it is God who acts through his sacramental promise. We react with joy and thanksgiving. You can relax and enjoy the start of a wonderful relationship begun in God's love; a relationship lived not only with your dear godchild, but a living relationship with your living God.

What Happens At The Baptism?

What you will hear during the sacrament is taken directly from the Bible, God's Word. You will hear the priest or pastor recall God's mighty deeds for his people and how water is involved in his saving acts for his people.

Examples of this are his Spirit moving over the waters of creation (Genesis 1:2), how the wicked were condemned in the Great Flood and Noah and his family were saved as chosen by God (Genesis 7 & 8), how Jesus was baptized in the waters of the Jordan River (Matthew 3:13) and how through the baptism of his own death and resurrection Jesus has set us free from the bondage to sin and death and has opened the way to the joy and freedom of everlasting life (Romans 6:4-5).

You will hear many words during the baptism. But you will also hear God's Word and be in the presence of the Word of God.

The Word of God is another way of saying, Jesus, God's Son, Our Lord. A handy way to think of this is that when God speaks, he doesn't speak mere words, God speaks things. In the beginning, when God created all that exists, God spoke, "Let there be light" and, "there was light (Genesis 1:3)." When God says he loves us, "the Word became flesh and dwelt among us . . ." That Word made flesh is Jesus, who was with God, and is God, from the beginning (John 1:14).

In the holy sacrament of baptism, we baptize the child or adult in the "name" of the one true God who comes to us in the three persons whom we recognize as the one God: Father, Son and Holy Spirit.

As we gather in God's Name, we gather in his powerful presence.

Before the actual baptism with water, you will probably recite a formula of the faith, the Apostles' Creed. You will tell everyone present that you believe in God the Father who created all there is; God the Son, Jesus who lived, and died for our sins and rose again from the dead; and God the Holy Spirit who convinces you of this truth and keeps you safely in the faith. You will profess belief in the "universal" or catholic Church, the communion of faithful people or "saints," the forgiveness of sin, the resurrection of the body and the life everlasting.

At the end you'll say, "Amen," which is an ancient way of saying, "That's right!"

Then the baptism will take place.

You will hear one of two formulas of baptism. One is from an ancient formula traditionally used by the Eastern church. It focuses on the active love of of God by keeping the priest or pastor a passive celebrant of God's active power. The formula is this: "John Matthew is baptized in the name of the Father, and of the Son, and of the Holy Spirit."

The Western church uses a formula that focuses more on the priest or pastor actively participating in the command of Jesus to, "Baptize all nations in the name of the Father and of the Son and of the Holy Spirit, teaching them to observe all I have commanded you (Matthew 28:19-20);" The celebrant in this formula proclaims, "John Matthew, I baptize you in the name of the Father, and of the Son and of the Holy Spirit."

In either formula, the emphasis is on God taking the initiative to promise his love to us and be our God so that we may be his people.

Suddenly, The Baptism Is Over —
And, Just Beginning

The big day has come and gone and now you realize its wonder. You have celebrated the fact of God's love for your godchild through the sacrament of holy baptism. The church has welcomed your godson or goddaughter into their family of faith as a fellow member of the Body of Christ and a worker with them in the kingdom of God.

But what happens now? Maybe you'll go out for lunch or have a party at home. But what happens later, next week or next month?

Jesus commanded his followers to, "teach them (all nations) all that I have commanded you . . . ." The church will have ways to keep in touch with your godchild. They will send him or her different educational materials suited to his or her age in order to keep the Lord's command and teach your godchild basic Christian truths. The church family will offer many ministries and activities centered on the love of God for your godchild. He or she will learn loving responses in order to share this divine love with his or her neighbor for the sake of the Lord.

You, too, will want to send your godchild Bible-based books, cards and letters to help him or her "abide in the Word," and be a faithful disciple of Christ (John 8:31). You will let him or her know the importance of Sunday school and church attendance.

You'll notice, dear godparent, that you are not responsible for the welfare of your godchild should his or her natural parents die. This is a common misunderstanding about being a godparent. Your relationship with your godchild is spiritual, not legal. Your responsibility is to continue your loving relationship with the parents and their child and to exercise your response-ability for the spiritual well-being of your godchild.

You are not a sponsor, nor a witness, nor a family friend at the baptism. You are to be a godmother or godfather to your godchild.

A Final Note

You have been given a great charge: to nurture and love your godchild in his or her spiritual well-being. God has acted in his divine love through Christ and his sacrament of baptism. And you are enabled to respond to his love with the Holy Spirit in your heart. You have been given a loving response-ability for God's child, your godson or goddaughter.

What can you do with your godchild to foster the loving response which God's love works in your godchild's heart?

1. If the child is an infant, ask to "babysit" for an evening and let the new parents rest from their hectic responsibilities.

2. Build something for the infant; a changing table, a mobile of simple Christian sayings to suspend over the crib.

3. Make a baptismal plaque or draw a baptismal certificate for your godchild's keepsake book. Include a montage of photographs taken at the baptism.

4. Read Bible "baby books" to your godchild. Learn the ABC's with Bible images, i.e., "A" is for ark. "B" is Bible. "C" is for Christ.

Here are some fun things to do which will enable the child to see his or her worth in God's eyes and share that worth with others. Most of these ideas will be fun and meaningful for an adult "godchild," too.

1. Attend a special festival service with your godchild and go out for lunch afterward.

2. Go to an exhibit of religious art at a local museum. Have a picnic, too.

3. Together watch a baptism at another church. Discuss the memories you have of your godchild's baptism.

4. Attend an outdoor spiritual retreat together. Find different forms of water, (rain, fog, ocean waves, dew, ponds, rivers, streams, your foggy breath on a chilly day). Then make a picture book about how water cleanses, refreshes, sustains life, and can be fun.

5. Draw pictures of a baptism in a river or baptismal font. Compare your pictures and comments about water and life.

6. Celebrate your godchild's baptismal birthday with his or her family and friends.

7. Sit with your godchild and his or her parents during church. Have lunch together as a "family."

8. Write occasionally to your godchild. Tell him or her about your own spiritual journey, the "ups and downs" of your faith, the meaning of your life and faith.

9. Pray daily for your godchild as you journey together following your Lord.

Basic Christian Beliefs

Finally, you will want to help your godchild in the "basics" of the Christian faith. You promised you would do this during the sacrament of holy baptism.

The basics are: The Lord's Prayer, the Apostles' Creed, the Ten Commandments, and instruction in the Holy Scriptures.

The last item, "instruction in the Holy Scriptures," is usually provided by Sunday school, church school or catechism class. Check with your pastor for details. Your godchild's natural parents will need to help here, too.

The Lord's Prayer, the Apostles' Creed and the Ten Commandments are included on the following pages to help you review them so you can practice them with your godchild.

THE LORD'S PRAYER

This prayer (Revised Standard Version of the Bible) to our heavenly Father is from the lips of Jesus as he taught us how to pray. It is a perfect prayer in praising God, trusting his will, telling him of our needs, asking him to help us to love others as he loves us, and praying that he keeps us safe and sound as his beloved children (Matthew 6:9-13).

Our Father in heaven,
hallowed be your name,
your kingdom come,
your will be done,
on earth as in heaven,
Give us today our daily bread,
Forgive our sins
as we forgive those
who sin against us.
Save us from the time of trial
and deliver us from evil.
For the kingdom, the power,
and the glory are yours,
now and forever. Amen.

THE APOSTLES' CREED

The Apostles' Creed is the basic belief-statement of a Christian church. It tells who God is and what he has done, will do, and indeed does for us each and every day for eternity. It is a personal belief-statement for each Christian to say. When you read this creed, read it out loud to hear your own voice declare who God is:

I believe in God, the Father almighty,
creator of heaven and earth.

I believe in Jesus Christ, his only Son, our Lord.
He was conceived by the power of the Holy Spirit
and born of the virgin Mary.
He suffered under Pontius Pilate,
was crucified, died and was buried.
He descended into hell
On the third day he rose again.

He ascended into heaven,
and is seated at the right hand of the Father.
He will come again to judge the living and the dead.

I believe in the Holy Spirit,
the holy catholic Church,
the communion of saints,
the forgiveness of sins,
the resurrection of the body,
and the life everlasting. Amen.

THE TEN COMMANDMENTS

The Ten Commandments were given to God's people from God. The Ten Commandments begin by God promising to be our God and then telling us what this promise entails within the loving relationship he establishes with us.

As we first noted in the discussion of holiness, Jesus summarized the Ten Commandments: You shall love the Lord your God with all your heart and with all your soul, and with all your mind. This is the great and first commandment. And a second is like it: You shall love your neighbor as yourself. On these two commandments depend all the law and the prophets (Matthew 22:37-40)."

1. I am the Lord your God, you shall have no other gods.
2. You shall not take the name of the Lord your God in vain.
3. Remember the Sabbath Day, to keep it holy.
4. Honor your father and your mother.
5. You shall not kill.
6. You shall not commit adultery.
7. You shall not steal.
8. You shall not bear false witness against your neighbor.
9. You shall not covet your neighbor's house.
10. You shall not covet your neighbor's wife or his manservant or his maidservant or his cattle or anything that is your neighbor's.

These Ten Commandments or, the Law, helps us to live orderly lives in full awareness of the needs of our neighbor. The Law also shows us our own weakness in keeping perfectly the Ten Commandments.

Because of our inability to keep God's law, we fail to love as we should, and are shown to be sinful. All sin deserves death because it separates us from God, who is love and life.

Thanks be to God that he sent his only Son to die for us so that our sins would not sentence us to death. His perfection is bestowed on us through his life, death, resurrection and the faith he gives us through the Holy Spirit.

Thanks be to God that he made baptism a gift for us, in order to join us to his forgiveness and eternal life in Christ Jesus.

Thanks be to God that now we live a life full of the baptismal hope and love God has for us in Christ through the Holy Spirit.

www.ingramcontent.com/pod-product-compliance
Lightning Source LLC
Chambersburg PA
CBHW071759020426
42331CB00008B/2323